Year

RIVER WOLTON

Year

366 poems

RIVER WOLTON

illustrated by
EMMA BURLEIGH

smith|doorstop

the poetry business

Published 2022 by The Poetry Business
Campo House,
54 Campo Lane,
Sheffield S1 2EG
www.poetrybusiness.co.uk

ISBN 978-1-914914-36-2
eBook ISBN 978-1-914914-56-0

Designed & typeset by Francesca Romano.
Printed by Mixam.

British Library
Cataloguing-in-Publication Data.
A catalogue record for this book is available
from the British Library.

Smith|Doorstop is a member of Inpress
www.inpressbooks.co.uk.
Distributed by IPS UK, 1 Deltic Avenue,
Rooksley, Milton Keynes MK13 8LD.

The Poetry Business gratefully acknowledges
the support of Arts Council England.

for my brother
Adam Allan Wolton
9 December 1964–26 November 2021

for my neighbour
Rob Slingsby
23 September 1982–20 March 2022

for my friend
Kate Hendickson
3 August 1990–17 April 2022

Contents

Foreword

River Wolton's year of poems on the theme of kindliness (*mettā*) touches the heart and invites us into friendliness, reminding us that softening and patience are possible. Each day River wrote a poem, a discipline in itself which could be inspiring for many. In doing that she invites us into her life, her practice of meditation, her reflection on the vagaries of feelings and events. Each poem is a jewel to be felt and meditated upon. The poems have different shapes and each feels fresh responding to the moment it is lived in.

This year of poetry is a poetic manual of meditation in action. It encourages us to practice mindfulness meditation in a friendly way. It shows us that mindfulness is more than observing and being present. For this observing and being present to make a difference as we encounter the ups and downs of life, it has to be imbued with friendliness and compassion. Many poems show us this essential turning point, which helps River to move from criticism and judgment to compassionate and caring acceptance.

2 January

Opening the door
    mid-grudge
and the touch of
    cool air
reminds me
    of the intention
    for befriending –
this too
    the sullen step
    the grating thought.

Meditation is not about being perfect
and serene in all circumstances
but about creatively engaging in
a kind and compassionate way
with inner and outer events and
moods. When this can happen there
is a possibility of softening and
flowing with what we encounter.
By softening inwardly we become
more open outwardly.

5 January

Admin:
the art
of not sinking under
tedium.

How to remember
the kind response
to self
and other.

In the woods,
winter Sunday walk,
the deer
have worn a new path.

River also encourages and shows us
how to let go.

4 February

The email treadmill
gaining speed
and me
pushing it along
frightened
of getting overwhelmed
in the backlog
and in the process
frightening
and overwhelming
myself.
How delicious
to give over.

River also reminds us of the tools a caring and careful mindfulness gives us to apply in our daily difficulties and pain.

This volume is inspiring and moving in many ways. It asks us to be present, to be kind, to be concerned, to be generous.

Martine Batchelor

5 February

Sometimes
in the midst of rage
the kindest thing
is to bring weight
to the feet
lean back into the heels
close eyes
and let the fire
burn itself out.

Introduction

On 1 January 2020 I made an intention to dedicate the year to mettā, the innate human capacity for kindness, goodwill and friendliness.* Not the saccharin cliché but the sort of kindness that includes its opposites and obstacles. I resolved to write a poem a day and not to shy away from the realities of irritation, ill will, rage and pettiness.

As Covid-19 came closer the poems turned to the pandemic and the landscapes of uncertainty, vulnerability and inequality that the virus revealed.

Gradually the daily practice of writing a poem began to build its own momentum. There were days when it seemed an impossible task: I felt too stressed, too wordless, too sick (from what I began to realise was Long Covid), and there were days when the poems arrived whole, as if of their own volition. The container and continuity of the intention held me. Each day after writing I read that day's poem from the previous month, and the ebb and flow of different weather patterns – inner and outer – washed over me.

Whatever the year and date you read this, I hope that something in this collection helps to remind you of what matters, and to spark your imagination.

River Wolton
Hope Valley
June 2022

*Mettā is from Pali, the language akin to Sanskrit in which early Buddhist philosophy and teachings were written down.

January

1 January

Who will come aboard this ship
as she weighs anchor and sets sail?
Who will come aboard?
The being's mean nooks,
tiresome habits, shadows?
Come aboard the ship of friendship
that risks setting its compass
through uncharted waters
towards kindness, towards love.

2 January

Opening the door
    mid-grudge
and the touch of
    cool air
reminds me
    of the intention
    for befriending –
this too
    the sullen step
    the grating thought.

3 January

A sunny day
draws me
to the garden.
Which is kinder –
to rake the leaves
or let them lie,
pull the weeds
or leave them?

4 January

A scant and brittle patience
with gnawing impatience,
a third helping,
the pull to numb
    and dull,
to despair.

5 January

Admin:
the art
of not sinking under
tedium.

How to remember
the kind response
to self
and other.

In the woods,
winter Sunday walk,
the deer
have worn a new path.

6 January

Rain eases at twilight
a grey herd of cumulus rolls to the west,
waxing moon and evening star
in a pearl-navy sky.

At the five-barred gate
the trees are beyond beauty.
I try not to hurry to the next thought

but offer what I can
to the soul whose shoulders bloom
with epaulettes of kindness.

7 January

Listening to my voice recorded
can I be gentle with the hesitations,
errs and umms? Dare myself to patience,
gather a protective cloak of imperfection
from the gaps and pauses.

8 January

Heart pounds forward
through night
as if body's both
desperate horse
and racetrack
no gentleness
for generations
only the bit
gritted teeth
wild endurance.

9 January

A moment or two
in between
doing and being
something and someone.
A moment or two
to walk back and forth
heel and toe
a slow dance step
in the busy buzzing.

10 January

I sleep less
and live on
chips and pasties
but the tiredness
means I listen
carefully
at chance encounters,
take in
the kind face
of the friend
of a friend
of a friend.

11 January

Slicing leeks
I notice
shoulders tensed
arms rigid;
bring ease
into the motion,
simply standing
at the kitchen counter,
oil heating in a pan,
nowhere to go.

12 January

Sun's gift
shears' gift
gift of birdbath
shimmering in light breeze,
gift of last year's robin's nest
in the hedge, gift of scraping leaves

add up to the gift of resting by the fence
giving full attention to my neighbour's
season of loss.

13 January

I cradle the warm almost-featherless chicken
and try to marry this tenderness
with the two point six million chickens
killed each day in this country alone

and with the line of people waiting
to collect hundreds of rescued chickens
and those who gently dole them out
in ones and twos and threes.

14 January

the alarm goes and goes
and after a while
becomes a cue ...
to begin the day with
may I be well and safe
may we all be well

15 January

Rain hurtles against obstacles,
a climate-change downpour.
Cold and soaked-through
I'm herding chickens.

Saturated with rage
I yell Enough!

Know anger as anger,
seek distraction:
lemon, honey, a lit stove.

16 January

Mercy has a thousand arms that curve
from right and left towards the sternum
like graceful, patient waiters
offering platters of comfort.

17 January

An ordinary day
of shelves
and pleasantries
then suddenly
a friend's bad news –
cancer returning.
The humdrum
fractures
and there's nowhere
to look
but here, this
strange and frail
thing of breath.

18 January

Where's kindness now?
A slight adjustment
a loosening
a pause
an out-breath to let
the relentless shears
of time and being gape.

19 January

Cusp of a cold bright day, cold night
and dusk is lit by liquid notes.
I pinpoint a robin in the hazel,
chest-feathers puffing out
with each snatched breath.
For a while everything else
kneels down and falls away.

20 January

New pain sears inside my left hip.
Somehow I remember to stretch,
sit awhile with the breath,
run a bath. Twenty years ago
I would have stayed asleep.

21 January

Cynicism
blocks the path:
'I am your one and only
how dare you dream
of abandoning me!'
We lock eyes.
I try to stand my ground.

22 January

Morning view
from the top of the track.

At evening I recall
this greenbrowngrey vista

the valley's white mist
like a sleeping dragon's breath.

23 January

Another sunny day,
premature snowdrops,
fragile bronze blossoms
on the witch-hazel.
I savour warmth
and sense the climate
changing.

24 January

to be honest
not a whole heap
of outstanding kindness
today
just the satisfaction
of ticking things
off the list

25 January

I'm listening out for
the voice
that says
you did OK
you can rest now
from the re-hashing,
give the noble weariness its due.

26 January

The bar's almost empty,
Ella's singing 'Stormy Weather',
I'm doing a crossword
with the bar staff
and the taste of
in-between and awaiting
with rain against the window
becomes everything.

27 January

The To Dos
are up and marching
from start to finish
but yes, there is a gap
to glance up
see
a treecreeper
plump as a mouse
zig-zag-hopping up
a silver birch.

28 January

Hassan in a Network Rail jacket
at Birmingham New Street
tends the disgorged passengers
as if we're nervous goats:
'Terminating here ...
incident on the line ...
buses to Cheltenham ...
wait here ... follow me ...'
repeated reassuringly
as we trundle after him
up escalators, across roads.

29 January

still air   new moon
Cassiopeia   Andromeda
mortality   infinity

offer   this   wonder
to the soul and humbly
offer this soul skywards

oh let there be space
between the nitpicketing
                compulsions

30 January

Shock and worry, worry and guilt
discerning where I've failed
and where I have been
powerless

Just how powerless I am
is both horror
and relief

Dare I let forgiveness
spread through
my skin?

31 January

here too
kindness for the
nervous, sweating
anticipating

here too
pausing
letting tenderness come

and the gunboats
of perfectionism
recede
into the dark

February

1 February

For a while
aligning with
compassion
inner, outer
coolness
spreading
like a lake
in the torso
a lake to dwell beside.

2 February

Bones exhausted
nerves jangling
trying, trying
for rest.

Lean back, dear one,
let the work be done.

3 February

Running in the morning lanes
falling forward with familiar rhythm
three strides to an out-breath

and held wherever I turn
by a cradle of birdsong.

4 February

The email treadmill
gaining speed
and me
pushing it along
frightened
of getting overwhelmed
in the backlog
and in the process
frightening
and overwhelming
myself.
How delicious
to give over.

5 February

Sometimes
in the midst of rage
the kindest thing
is to bring weight
to the feet
lean back into the heels
close eyes
and let the fire
burn itself out.

6 February

hurrying
on irritation's road
nothing
going the right way

7 February

The kindness of the dentist
and the dental nurse
as the tooth numbs up
before extraction.

8 February

The critic storms in
with banners flying:
Mediocre!
Irrelevant!
Incompetent!
The best I can do
is sigh, affirm
the beauty
of something
being past
and therefore
irredeemable.

9 February

Was it for this the clay grew tall?
  – Wilfred Owen

A break in torrential rain
and lashing wind; I walk up
the flooded boggy lane
to the field where two birches
splintered in the storm; fragile
the earth, fragile these outcrops
of which we're clumsy guardians.

10 February

Driving back in the dark
I switch off the radio and tune in
to compassion's wavelength;
hands loosen on the wheel,
and in the headlights
trees become mythical.

11 February

After hours of procrastination
while hail rattles the window
and snow flecks the view,
I turn to the dreaded task
and find it is, in moments, possible
when freed from the stories
I've been telling.

12 February

I wake early and flounder
heart pounding as waves collide
in frothing confusion; no adequate
reply to their accusations.

13 February

No recollection
of the early morning walk
except streams
criss-crossing the track
a slew of mud
and Kinder Scout
laced with snow.

14 February

Mood plummets
like a barometer
before the storm
and little to remedy it
save a warm bath,
a side-step towards patience,
and – fingers in ears –
seascape of breath.

15 February

(after *Parasite*)

The film replays
its horrors
till I wake before dawn

the flood's torrenting
down walls and stairs
into basements.

Head out up the hill
stumbling defiant
against rain and mud.

While I can still run
I'll run.

16 February

Rain hammers through the night.
Flood warnings in place.
There's a trailer of sandbags
in the council car park.
I drive past guiltily to buy
air-freighted lettuce
wrapped in plastic,
skirt water, shiny tarmac,
deluged fields, the depth
of what we're losing.
Then tears come
as offers of help pour in
on the village WhatsApp.

17 February

A morning like many others –
flat weight of a clouded,
airless heart. You have wasted
your life. Try to breathe –
any help will do, warmth of sheet
and bed. Forget mid-way.

18 February

Watch morning clouds blow west to east
then chomp through the hours.
Brief glimpse of a clear night sky –
Orion's Belt, plane's tail-lights.

19 February

Outside the solicitor's window
and what is hard to bear –
two winter trees;
all day I'm held in their arms
see things from their point of view,
the honest branches
        clouds
                the city sky.

20 February

one conscious out-breath
and the poem
        appears

21 February

All day running
with the thought
'I'll attend to this pain
later'.

22 February

An old friend phones, despite
a thousand challenges all's ended well.
Alhamdulillah, Alhamdulillah!
Delight like a heaped plate
shared under a gentle sun.

23 February

Restless night and pelting dreams
yet morning brings a question:
what if I was diligent caretaker
of this jangling body I call my own?

I move about and practise patience
as if I believed it, as if doubt
was not always the sole trader here.

24 February

Good news comes
amid bouts of rain
and ceaseless wind
I press the phone
to my ear
and my head
to the window.
Can it be true
after so long?
Shock re-sets
the world
leaves me winded
with joy.

25 February

Despite stringent planning
I utterly mistime the session
but
there's barely any
punishment or blame.

26 February

Drawing the blind
I glimpse the north star
pared silver of new moon
navy-blue sky.

27 February

Reprieve for dear J
today is not the last.
The message spreads time open
like a fan; I eat slowly
then go outside
to cut down bracken,
lay it over muddy ground.

28 February

Snow then rain
on saturated earth,
wordless grief rises.
I can't do this life.
Try to be a soft container
inches from the skin,
let the falling keep falling
till it falls apart.

29 February

Late night
early morning
a little precious sleep
tears help
and the beloved's arms;
carried by prayer
and practice
moving through
what must be seen
and done.

March

1 March

Criticism comes
out of the blue
like driven hail
in the face
feel the sting
the wounding
to the self
who wants to get it right
to help
to be all things
to everyone.

2 March

Bumbling home
along the dark track
oblivious of water on stone,
the patient trees;
but when I'm nearly there
the half-moon sheds her cloud mantle
above next door's chimney stack.

3 March

Dad would have been 119 today.
I remember him in daffodils,
cherry blossom, ridged nails
cracked like his, thin skin.

4 March

Let me be forgiven for the strange
and partial things I utter
when under pressure
or in the grip of thinking
I need to know it all.
Let those who listen
not think less of me.
For time's too short
to dwell another minute
in the house of shame.
And there's sunshine
to soothe the back
and clear hill-streams
to rinse muddy wellies
after a long walk home.

5 March

Working into the evening
fuelled by a handful
then a whole bag
of chocolate mini-eggs.

6 March

The tender lifeguard of the soul
remembers the option
of an afternoon nap.

7 March

Allowing something
to be less than perfect
        – much less –
is like a golden thread
wrapped around the moment,
a gift for the future.

8 March

Just after six
the phone rings –
J has died.
Expected news
and still the shock,
this breath,
this bite, this sip.
Ten days ago
I messaged
with good news,
her generous delight
returned immediately.
She's everywhere –
in those last WhatsApp emojis,
her painting of the swan's full flight,
her face in mind's eye.
Everywhere : nowhere.

9 March

Soon after waking
I remember that she's died
and push into the hurt
to check it's real.
All day I listen
relentlessly
to coronavirus.

10 March

Reconciled to
being under-the-weather
means I slump more
find a low note
of deep rest

try to speak from the back –
shoulder-blades, spine, ribs –
rather than the eager clavicles
who think they should know it all
and soon.

11 March

Bearing witness to trauma and injustice
I remember to weight the heels
stretch awareness to make room
for the smouldering fires of rage.

12 March

Is it kinder to hear as many bulletins as possible
                    – or not –
to keep abreast of the virus, to stay on the live edge
of radical uncertainty?

13 March

What if every day
was like the birthday
of the beloved –
the impetus
to act from generosity
to say
'It's your day
you can choose'
so little to choose
when we open
to the virus
bearing down,
but the lark
captures our attention
with her ecstatic song
and descent
to the field
where our eyes
strain to see her
and her work
is done.

14 March

Ms Grumpy close at hand
rattled by constant Covid talk
and handwashing.
But celebrating with the choir
lifts the clouds till
she can't help but smile.

15 March

There is coronavirus
and there is the sky
the shallow waterfalls
of Lathkill Dale
two swans preening
wild white violets
a dipper flitting
from rock to depths.

I've read so much news
I feel unwell.

Grateful for stopping
at twilight
to listen to calm words
grateful for awareness
that can be the ground
where everything unfolds.

16 March

Can I be a gentle guardian
to this one
who returns my gaze
in the mirror?

17 March

virus of primroses
virus of blackbirds
        of raindrops
        of grass blades and puddles

18 March

Pushing against illness
(is it the virus?)
pushing through
to get things done
and blot out,
I realise now,
the shock.

19 March

A neighbour asks for help, hating, she says
to ask, ever, anyone.
I try to tell her the request is like a gift,
we are all desperate to help.

20 March

Through a gap in the trees I spot a big yellow skip
and speculate on the neighbour's building project,
then slowly realise it's a riotous bank of forsythia.

21 March

Fear, loss, the expanding uncertainties
bring this moment into clarity –
hawthorn's new emerald leaves,
primrose's pale-butter petals.

22 March

I garden in sunlight
and avoid the news.
Pruning dead wood
from the lavender
a splinter lodges
deep inside my thumb
which throbs
and swells. The world
narrows to a square
centimetre.

23 March

Early morning online meditation
with five hundred souls and then
I go to work, which is to walk
in sun-specked woods and hear
the first chiffchaff. These days
are ringed with urgency and pause.

24 March

Mid-meeting (screen of screens)
a long-tailed tit outside the window
flits off carrying a feather
twice her body's length.

The birds aren't in lockdown,
they're building nests
in the grand space
that is not Covid-19.

25 March

Quiet gets quieter,
birdsong louder,
a curlew's whistle-warble,
then a pair, their wings
unfurl like solemn sashes.
I stay away from news.

26 March

At eight o'clock the clapping starts
and even on our bumpy lane
neighbours stand outside or open windows
to applaud the NHS. In other streets
and cities there are fireworks,
in Rotherham someone plays
'Simply the Best' at full volume.

27 March

for some
lockdown
fuels
a hell realm

listening
to a friend
chest tightens
lungs constrict

28 March

I keep the news at bay
but it seeps in,
deaths escalate,
each statistic
someone
who could not be held
by those they loved.
In the midst of it
a radio programme
about the Rex Cinema Elland
where tea is served
in real mugs
and Mildred
the interval organist
plays till everyone's
had ice-cream.
'When all this is over'
we say, 'When all this ...'

29 March

A bitter wind
replaces days
of ridiculous sun.
We run against it
trying to block thoughts
with breath and sweat.

31 March

Heart jangles
like a church bell
yanked repeatedly
out of time.

Worry scours body.
No resting place
but swaddled
in a duvet.

30 March

What's here:
the pink-gold limbs
of silver birch.
Nothing where or how
it ought to be.

April

1 April

Taking refuge in the earth
(or at least the sofa cushions).
It may not be the true dharma
but velour is comforting.

2 April

Longing for a doorway to distraction
that a thirty-minute solitary walk
or a face on a screen
can't give.

I'm glad for a shared bed,
shared meal
and almost forgive her
for sneezing on the soup.

(Remember this
when it's all over,
how petty we became,
how loving.)

3 April

Life is both on edge
and crazily gentle

– the flowering currant thick with bees
a kestrel tilting between silver birch –

then it contracts in a second
to a bicker, a jaw-snap.

4 April

How did I do?
Should I have said this or that?

Meanwhile a pair of coal tits
in the hedgerow
chase spring's fierce dilemma.

Meanwhile Ptolemy the tortoise
wakes after five months' hibernation.

5 April

The silent road to Stanage
a few cyclists, other runners,
walkers, keeping our distance
but friendlier than usual.

What is usual
will it come again?

Two curlews call across the moor,
forget-me-nots splash blue
over the garden.

7 April

Giant moon, sunset beyond Kinder,
the rare glimpse of a plane's tail-lights.
Still the news is real and surreal,
still the roads are quiet – a waking dream,
a childhood memory.

6 April

I'm Zoom-sick
and walk for longer than I should,
revelling in three dimensions –
fields of pregnant sheep,
a dipper singing
across the Derwent.
Breathe in for the confined,
breathe out for the dying.

8 April

900 UK deaths today.
Grief erupts in hurt, blame,
waves of tiredness.

It's crazily hot
but I forget to walk.
What kindness now?

Sponging Ptolemy's shell –
he's awake three days,
nibbling dandelions.

9 April

Curlew mid-morning
thrush song at dusk.
Between the two –
screens, calls, plans,
the world's chaos

and some minutes
sitting on a rock
in the chicken field
looking out
across the valley.

10 April

We walk beside the placid river
to a shady bench
with ramsons, violets.

Geese slam the water
in a vicious courting dance,
snake-necks hissing,

like we've happened on a riot
in an empty valley.

11 April

The day stretches out beyond exhaustion
hundreds of faces on screens,
adrenalin of scrabbling for the next right words
or letting them rise to the surface like bright fish.
The unfamiliar joy of embodied
two-dimensional community.

12 April

Early morning field:
a ewe dead in labour,
new-borns, dew,
crows picking wool-clots
to line their nests.

13 April

Speaking into a screen
and trying not to watch
my own face
speaking back at me.
No matter how I try
to Hide Self View
it pops up again.
Hardly believing
that our voices travel
to Argentina, Australia.
Fortunate life
to have such magic in it.

14 April

We're brought again to love.
Even Boris Johnson speaks of it,
nursed through the dark in ICU
by Portuguese and New Zealand nurses.

Meanwhile borders are reinforced,
people handcuffed onto deportation flights,
immigration detention centres
locked down indefinitely.

15 April

Waking before the sun
nauseous and feverish
but alert enough
to sit with the breath
as grey lightens,
the dawn chorus begins,
and the heart
lays down its weapons
for now.

16 April

Twilit fields, mauve sky,
skittery lambs,
fractious ewes,
bats like fleeting snaps of night,

and Venus queen of love
a small bright stab of heaven
presiding as she should
over these months.

17 April

Walking after dark
under bruised clouds
remnants of orange
layered over Kinder.
'It's so unreal' you say
as we crane our necks
knowing it's not the sky
you mean.

18 April

Five stags emerge
from bracken and birch,
a wren chirrups across the lane.
Lambs and sheep
in two-tone octaves,
then we hear owls.
We don't see badgers
only mouths of setts.

Later a Horizon special
on coronavirus:
snakes writhing in mesh bags,
cages of chickens, pigs,
a rabbit gnawing metal.
And a small brown bat
one thousand heartbeats
to a minute.

19 April

Thank God
for a great documentary
about a good man
where all ends well.

20 April

After several days' absence
I walk to the lambing field
and hear the first cuckoo.

In the space between sounds
I think about human shields:
nurses, doctors, shelf-stackers,
delivery drivers.

It's not acceptable
for a self-respecting poet
to use the word 'heartbreak'
yet here it is.

21 April

Fears build and boil
till they spill into grief
for old loss and new,
the day is hammer-bright
leached dry by stop-start wind,
I walk about looking at spring
through plate-glass windows.

22 April

Listening to a friend's sorrows
and telling her mine. Thirty years
entwined. I do the best I can
her voice on speaker
sitting outside
where the signal's stronger
and trees are visibly greening.

23 April

Two lambs recline
on the path and I detour
to avoid them. Imagine
you'd the one green carpet –
food, mattress, toilet,
labour ward, death bed.
These parched days
make miracles of
grass, buttercups,
the eight o'clock samba band
of neighbours' saucepans,
the crazy fact
that we are here at all.

24 April

Running up that hill
reminded that
Kate Bush is a genius.

25 April

The unending violence done to women
in kindness' name; the great
and small harms – sugar, spice, all things nice –
make me want to rip these pages.

Blows form in fists.
I've walked this battleline,
it rises and it glows
I hear its thirst.

With the fight comes grief
that will not be consoled
or parted
from its creed of rage.

26 April

A friend's been to Leicester
for a job interview as a carer.
She speaks of the journey
as a wondrous adventure,
empty platforms, no ticket collector,
the carriage with one other passenger.
We lean in to the screen and listen
as if hearing about time travel
or walking through walls.

27 April

It takes weeks of lockdown
before I resort to dusting
and even then, doubt rules the day.

Walk and let the eyes travel over
cropped grass, sheep-shit, leaves.

I'm moving forward as I must
but there's no love in it.

28 April

For the first time in six weeks
I drive into the city.
It's like a rainy bank-holiday night

except for black and yellow tape
marking two metres
outside and inside shops.

I relish the lack of traffic,
the luxury of mobility
and forgetting.

29 April

Mood falls like the temperature
and there's plenty to push it lower
even without the news.

30 April

Plastic bag snagged on brambles:
peace flag or surrender.
I've forgotten everything I know
except this. This.

May

1 May

Run to the top.
Rain, sun, rain.
Who the hell do you think you are?

2 May

A long walk with friends
where gradually we stop distancing
and wind up on the station platform
with beer and scones
laughing at nothing
until the tannoy voice cuts in:
'Stay home, save lives.'

3 May

Seeing loved ones in the flesh again
we grin incurably across the distance
and forget how to make small talk.

4 May

A blackbird wakes me into presence;
4.53 p.m. I'm stomping through the woods
searching for Mary Oliver's ghost
but she's stopped speaking to me.

On and on the blackbird calls
from her blossom throne
while I lumber back and forth.
The rain begins.

Sometimes it's enough
to see hatred for what it is
and sometimes only time
and birdsong can erode it.

5 May

The swifts are back,
early morning, feathers rustle
as one enters the eaves' nest.
I sit in bed and watch
four sculpt the day.
Whose joy –
theirs-mine-theirs?

6 May

Millstones hold wall
trees hold sky
footsteps hold breath
and even holding
is a point of view:
a strange word
now I come to think of it,
by turns comfort
or restraint.

7 May

Great moon rises
like a dazzling silver tortilla.
Is this conviction, myth,
or intuition?
'Perception is malleable'.
In memory: Rob Burbea,
may you rest in peace.

8 May

VE day and what is the pandemic
doing to war-children locked-down,
girls who'll never return to school,
too many mouths to feed.

Will they be sold, or married young.
In Senegal, Afghanistan,
in South Sudan, remember those
whose freedom will be taken.

9 May

I dream we're banqueting
outside locked theatre doors,
miming in boxes, on screens,
so greedy I can't recognise myself,
confused as if it's going out of fashion.

11 May

A stint in the community shop, waiting
for customers, wrapped to the nines,
watching *Planet of the Humans* on my phone
and eyeing up unnecessary items.

10 May

I see the hare before it sees me
running headlong
on collision course

stock-still I've a second
to take in its lolloping
secret fearlessness

then it startles, veers off,
vanishes.

12 May

Nostalgic for lockdown
I bumble about, lost and incompetent.

Follow the swifts at dusk
twilight cuckoo, single plane
a speck that could be satellite.

13 May

Lifting my phone
to snap the picture
I miss the moment
when the owl
perched on the barn
takes flight.

14 May

A thousand bows to friendship
that's weathered decades
and listens while I blame into the phone,
suggests solutions, finds the funny side.

15 May

'And they all lived
happily ever after'
you murmur
as we watch another
lockdown haircut
on YouTube
before taking up
the clippers.

16 May

When in doubt
find a good field
to scrat about in.

17 May

Curlew, roe deer, cuckoo.
Bless the impulse calling me to rise and run at dawn.

18 May

Cuckoo at Bole Hill quarry.
One hundred years ago
a million tons of stone
hauled down this slope
to build the Derwent dams.
Now fierce song fills it,
holds us up.

19 May

Sorrow comes again
butting through disguises
then on to its frontiers and silences.
Still there's no rain,
the twilight lengthens
and beaks a symphony
of small tongues.

20 May

What do we know –
big-brained two-legged ones
with our sweated formulations,
immense labours?

Two young stags
in the chicken field
unclothe from hedgerow's shade,
antlers velvet, glowing.

21 May

Driving to and fro
listening to a climate scientist:
lockdown reduced emissions
three to seven percent
but what, she says,
about the other ninety?
I devour crisps
and try to get my head
around degrowth.

22 May

Another night I lie awake
to the heart drumming
as the dance partners
of impatience and anxiety
plod their monotonous routine.
The hours eke by.

23 May

and finally
I tidy
the potting shed

24 May

Eid Mubarak.

Sunday afternoon in Crookes Valley
we watch the canoeist
capsize and right himself repeatedly
under clouds which could be
horses, frogs or whales.

25 May

nausea and chills
no appetite
I flop in a deckchair
on a sunny bank holiday
swathed in a blanket

26 May

We drive to a carpark
outside Buxton,
squaddies in desert camouflage
drop a test on the back seat.

I scoop at my tonsils
trying not to retch
or stare at other drivers
peering down their throats
in rear-view mirrors.

I've read far too much
about Dominic Cummings.

27 May

Nausea and screens rule the day.

28 May

Snapshots:

a dreamt heap of gleaming coins

the loyal blackbird's recital

two deer-shaped shadows

potatoes grated for rösti

the *Guardian* crossword online

moths

four notes from the cuckoo

a walk to the gate

dizzy spells

the test result: negative.

29 May

George Floyd

speak his name

30 May

I dream I'm possessed
and only knotted blue amulets
can free the demons.

Waking, I remember
freedom's not transcendence

much as I'm driven to leave,
to get away once and for all.

31 May

10 p.m. The blackbird
works its repertoire,
I want to compare it
to something else –
a chuckle, a wild trill,
an abandon –
but attempt to stay
the sweet side of unknowing
hearing the sound
pour out in phrases
I'll never grasp.
If I could stay here
I'd dissolve.

June

1 June

On her birthday Cee and I
watch three ravens mob a buzzard,
a treecreeper on a Corsican pine.
We speak of the bird of prey
that no-one must speak of
lest it be hunted down,
and how much louder
everything is now.

2 June

running downhill
the last thought
is of mindfulness and social class
then my trainer catches a stone
I'm outstretched headlong bang knee
elbow grazed and bloody
I lie in the dust crying
then hobble home

3 June

Still limping I keep busy
but this evening sitting
with our group of teens and mentors
guided by Kareem's wise words,
grief rises at centuries of racist killing
oceans of young lives lost,
the lie that it only happens 'over there'.

4 June

Waking in pain
I wrap my arms around my bony shoulders
recall the ship of kindness,
slowly hoist the sail.

5 June

first takeaway
    since lockdown –
we over-order
    watch half of it grow cold

6 June

In deserted cities
thousands gather
masked and kneeling
Black Lives Matter.

7 June

A mistake to look at Twitter,
for all the courage
there are swathes of hate.
A twilight walk in oak woods:
wordless sorrow.

8 June

Never under-estimate the mind's capacity
to construct mountain ranges
from the dust of worry,
gravel of assumptions.

9 June

Triggered by men's voices
violent heat
is pulsing through my arms.

There may come a time
to plant forgiveness
but for now I pin my gaze

listen for fledglings
stand beside anger
not chivvy it to change.

10 June

    to sit in silence
to start the day
    by stopping
in company of others
    albeit on a screen
is to begin well
    no matter that thoughts dither and fret
is to begin
    again

11 June

under low rolling cloud
despite the freight train's thunder
a blackbird's dusk elegy
from the flailing topmost branch

above all
birdsong got me through

12 June

birdsong got me through
and more episodes of *Queer Eye*
than I care to admit

in the rain the lanes are silent
I've gone nowhere
for five days

well and good to meditate
on friendliness
but I miss actual friends

linking arms as we walk
holding hands

13 June

Streets full, shops busier,
irritation sparks at queues,
at those who cross my path
and take too long deciding.

This is where patience wakes –
not in long hours of studying clouds
but in stepping back and pausing
while someone cuts across
to reach for the tomatoes.

14 June

Five goldfinches peck thistle seed
beside the inner ring road,
an afternoon to mourn
spewed binbags and discarded masks

and with a seven-year-old
delight at seagulls soaring over tower blocks
with clouds of jellyfish and puppies
on the sky's great screen.

15 June

but the wasps' nest

I bury it
   (too close to the door
    a risk to visitors)
and watch them
pitch their bodies
against mountains

they've but one season
I begrudge them that

16 June

Marcus Rashford
with dignity & grace
forces a U-turn
from the government
on free school meals

17 June

I don't know why I'm crying in the woods
or forever hungry

or trying to take charge
of what's beyond my reach

can there be forgiveness
from inside collapse

18 June

At four a.m.
the shift from rage to hate
gets clear

the fire focuses
becomes a burning arrow
seeks a target

double-ended barb
pierces their belly
and mine

19 June

Juneteenth

Trump is rallying in Oklahoma
for a while I wish him dead

then remember lines of fake tan
trickling down his face

20 June

opening the door
on how my mind
has been both colonised
and coloniser
opening to a tide
and fleets of shame
ready to plant flags

21 *June*

On the longest day
we walk after dark,
a plane's tail-lights blink
and disappear
in thick cloud to the west,
minutes later
you spot a glow-worm
in the bracken.

22 *June*

Blinding sunshine's here again
the swifts circle and shriek.
I nurse fatigue, sore throat,
headache and wonder
whether to take another test.
Temperatures in the Arctic
hit an all-time high.

23 *June*

I sell seven large bars of Dairy Milk,
five bottled waters, four honeycomb ice-creams
and just before closing two bananas, two satsumas,
two pears 'for a fruit salad'.

We walk in sunset's thick air
hot as a foreign summer.
New moon underscored by curlew
and bats' soft flickering.

24 *June*

No escape from soaring heat
or wanting something.
Except a few minutes
under birch and hazel
to be thoroughly glad
not to live – yet –
in a land without shade.

25 June

Teetering on kindness' cusp:
to stop or carry on,
to narrow or broaden focus,
to pause
or strike while the iron's hot.
Everything stifling hot just now
sung heroes of night and breeze.

26 June

Nausea and heat combine
to make the day come from left field
as if I woke not fitting the frame
a half-step to the side of my life.

I get out the sewing machine
and become a person
who pins fabric
and loads bobbins with thread.

27 June

The swifts hatch
their hungry squeaks
begin at our bedroom window
and the parents' loyal shadows
swoop to and fro
despite the thunderclouds.

28 June

waking early
in pain
can I
turn with
care
to
the ageing body

I slip between patience
and not, between
befriending
and denial,
between chips
and chocolate

29 June

foxglove flowers
against the lime bouquet
of lady's mantle
pause in rainy dusk
sup nourishment
before onwards
to maybe easing
or local lockdown
and many other
hapless unknowns

30 June

Watching James Baldwin
'I Am Not Your Negro'
layers of white conditioning
rise to the surface
like blistered paint.

July

1 July

begins with nausea.
Split seconds of softening,
how close can tenderness land?
Surface layer or further in
towards the core of this
worried, forgetful one?

I give out facemasks.
Nothing will be the same.

2 July

Walking to the chicken field
grey air laced with honeysuckle.
Can the scent of friendliness
infuse these days
as change bombards us?

3 July

What is well?
copper beech canopy,
swift fledglings, wild strawberries,
Paracetamol, a hand to hold, the cat by the fire.

4 July

Body aches and staggers.
At times I tend to it
at times ignore it
lifting too-heavy loads
running here and there.

5 July

Toasting marshmallows
in the fire bowl
rain dribbling down our backs
we borrow a seven-year-old's
appetite for adventure
the cold and wet recede
and soon we're off again.

6 July

Why years of austerity
when billions are (so it seems)
pulled from thin air?
Ideology makes for fools
and hunger.

But with only a drop of news,
the afternoon sunny
and pain lessening – hallelujah –
mind brightens,
finds byways of delight.

7 July

Even as rain turns from shower
to downpour
and the heating comes on
for the first time in weeks
there is also yellow vetch,
a customer's smile,
a blackbird chattering up the path,
a hot-water bottle.
Small things adding up,
pointing the way.

8 July

Praise the gentle company of ruminants,
their single-mindedness.

9 July

The walk nearly over
I pull back the hood
tilt my face to the drizzle
surprised at how softly it lands.

Sounds flood in
from hill and thicket,
wren, blackbird, curlew;
a swallow flicks between tree-tops.

If fear was this easy to dismantle
how lightly we'd live,
courage raining its clear touch
on the body's earth.

10 July

little to show
except tasks completed
and my back warming
in dappled sun

11 July

Dreaming so deeply
it takes time to surface
to recall where, when, how
but then we drive to Sainsbury's
past open pubs
and the streets seem
almost ordinary.

12 July

witnessing violence
breath shakes
solar plexus judders
for hours afterwards
muscles berate their
immobility
I curse myself
for missing any chance
I might have seized
to say No

13 July

First time in four months
I enter someone else's house

Cross the threshold
Almost formal

Rush-hour traffic
Almost normal

I cook and eat
Prayerfully

As if I could put the brakes on

14 July

Choosing the twilight walk
over another round of Netflix;
low rolling cloud, bats,
my hand keeping warm
in your pocket.

15 July

I sit reading in the community shop
so quiet
a blackbird, beak dripping with worms
hops through the open door
to check if there's anything useful
for her hungry second brood.

16 July

here and there
remembering
to lean in
to a taste
a sound
the weight of the foot
and the next step

17 July

fifteen, twenty swifts
giddy and soaring
as we eat outside
clouds ablaze to the west
to the east

18 July

Eating cake with friends
two metres apart in the rain.
A birthday like no other
but for once resting back
no place to go.

19 July

Mum would have been ninety-five today.
Would she recognise us
hurtling to climate breakdown?
Once I thought she could fix anything,
Limits to Growth on the bookshelf.

20 July

My system aches
in new and frightening ways.
Early morning I attempt
to soften to the pain
meeting familiar obstacles.
Cultivating ease
by no means easy.

21 July

Sleepless nights, lacklustre days
and as the weeks swim by
the mirage of
an Ultimate Place of Safety
shimmers beyond reach.

Yet also in an outbreath
fists loosen as the body lands
in this one wholehearted
fleeting, ceaselessly moving
now.

22 July

Something's killed a pigeon
eviscerated it and left it on the path.
Flies buzz around the entrails and plucked skin.
I pick it up and hurl it over the fence
before the chickens are drawn to the blood.

For a second its entire weight and wingspan
hangs from my thumb and forefinger.

23 July

I'm almost used to masks
but not to the novelty
of sitting outside a café with Helen
in the sun, eating the best ever
cheese and tomato toastie.
We walk through Rivelin Valley,
families navigate the stepping-stones
and dogs splash after them.

24 July

Day of opposites:
gathered – scattered
sun – downpour

in the gaps
broad brushstrokes
of despair

through it all
weave aching limbs
and weariness.

25 July

Nausea stands with me as I stand
follows my footsteps
hovers while I drink and eat.

I google symptoms.
Post-Covid? Long Covid?

I'm trying hard to listen
but I get static, crossed wires,
old earworms.

26 July

A threadbare night
patched with scant sleep
so that I teeter through the day
fall into tasks I've long delayed –
needle and thread, hoovering the rug,
washing a blanket. A muzzy but tidier version
of myself.

27 July

Monday morning city centre
empty rain-slicked pavement,
sanitiser at each door,

stress shoots to the fore:
'What have you to show
for all these lazy months?'

28 July

Sitting on a rock at the field's edge
I watch the ewe stagger to her feet and limp
then kneel and lie down again
chewing any grass within reach.

In the seeing only the seeing.

The rock, the path home, the shrubs
the absence of chiffchaffs, of wren,
the aching bones, the stumble.

All resting on each other, indefinable.

29 July

Yesterday I found Hildegard the hen foraging in a neighbour's
field. She seemed content to be picked up and cradled home,
head bobbing between tall bracken. I set her in the run, scattered
mealworms, found the egg laid in her secret nest.

Lately she's roamed further, wild nature growing stronger, not stick-
ing with the flock.

Today I carry her stiff body, gather handfuls of down. The fox
has torn a blooded rent in her back. Grief flails against undoable
conditions – the domestication of woodland fowl, the breeding of
almost-flightless birds, the co-evolving of predator and prey

and Hilde, defying anything that could contain her.

30 July

warm evening
almost full moon
honeysuckle
stippled sky
dark-green shadows
I keep it all
at arm's length
so as not to become
a walking tree
a cloud fading

31 July

dashing here, there, up, down
a moment to think
'This is stress'
before continuing
to run and pour and chop
and light and stir

August

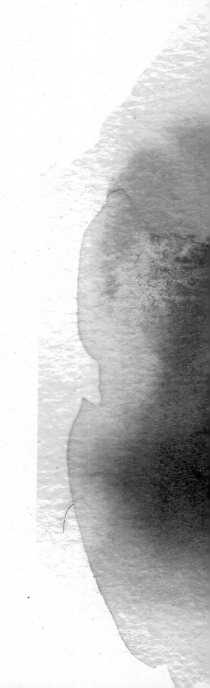

1 August

Headache, naps,
and trying, trying
to tune to kindness
for this tired,
wayward mind.

2 August

Grateful to run
grateful for eggs
for trains and the playground
for the outdoor swimming pool open again
grateful for standing-on-one-leg competitions
to lighten frustration at queuing,
for the kids' delight
at being in the water.
Grateful for walking home
along the river,
grateful for questions
and roast cabbage,
grateful for a clean bed
to hold the weary bones
and aching head.

3 August

Listening to Resmaa Menakem I realise
anew how dearly I want to be
a good white person
but 'good' is not
compassionate
non-violent
truthful
honest
awake.

4 August

While I looked away the swifts fledged.
Now they're flying south 6,000 miles
and will not land again till they return.
Fierce wind topples the tomato plants.
I wrap up, fill a hot-water bottle,
seek comfort in a weird season.

5 August

Listening to news of the Beirut explosion
and more: a measureless ocean of suffering.
Mind moves towards and away, towards, away,
remember, forget, remember, pray.

6 August

9.15 p.m. at the five-barred gate:
trees pitch-perfectly still,
a bat and another,
fine chisel of wren's call,
last bumblebee, first owl;

the world's in little need of this breath,
what in heaven can I offer –
strange, small witness
whose heart breaks
even for the passing clouds.

7 August

Walking meditation
and the garden becomes
something other than chores left undone –
hawthorn, hoverflies, wood pigeon cooing.
Palate flooded with abundance on this evening
of the hottest day in decades, the balmy air receives
and tremors with the depth of fear, the breadth of mourning:
nothing that can't be held.

8 August

A day of glory –
sunflies and ladybirds,
with yellow vetch and selfheal
spreading through tall grass –

and of grief –
complicity with racism,
illusion of the good white person
crumbling.

9 August

Homemade Yorkshire puddings –
another first from these months.
I love their every-which-way shape
ballooning from confinement.

10 August

After the day's heat
I walk the humid, dusty lane.
Freight train booms through
the valley – nothing muffles
the sound's full weight.

A snippet of six o'clock news –
Antarctic's melting ice sheets
are visible from space.
Dread burns the heart,
courage, don't desert me.

11 August

Rushing and rushing to arrive
then pausing, stopping,
rushing, hurrying,
busy, nothing,
and beginning
all over again.

12 August

Persistent and reliable
is the hand that keeps cranking out
the earworm.

Three weeks and counting.

Someone's making it spin,
if I could name her would she be
the one who trembles to descend,

to inhabit without question
this contingent, over-heated
bag of skin?

13 August

A little cooler today,
fidgets and firearms
less primed to take aim
though I point and shoot
video of the stag
scraping its antlers
against saplings.
Is it that time of year again,
time to shed, to be done
with the unwieldy burden?

14 August

Late-night Netflix
soothes in the moment
but colours my dreams
with foreboding.

15 August

Listen to a programme
on how the 1918 pandemic
changed the world –
for worse, for better –
and how quickly
despite good intentions
despite waking up
we fall asleep again.

16 August

Learning tall grasses after decades of walking through them,
pulling their stalks and chewing the ends.
     Quake
          Yorkshire Fog
               Wavy Hair-grass
    Common Bent
        Tall Oat Grass
            Soft Brome
glistening in heavy rain, dignified
as all things should be by being named.

17 August

Morning drizzle and low cloud
but as I walk into the hare field
a dozen swallows sift the mist,
tilt pale bellies to the yellowing birch.
More swallows than I've seen for years
rise and skim the bracken.
This is what brings me to the valley,
what saves me day on day.

18 August

First home-grown fig ripens
from the bud that set a year ago.
Sweet purple flesh
inside a green lightbulb
that's withstood torrents,
blizzards, hail.

Plants can't move
only adapt or die.
In the fig's elbows and armpits
tiny new fruit takes shape.

19 August

Jogging up the lane
no breeze, bracken starting to fold
and yellow, the warm, apple-y smell
of decay.

20 August

Higger Tor, purpling heather
and the true blue
cloud-spun sky.

We snuggle in the rock's curved seat
yesterday's deluge shining
in gritstone dimples.

From here the edges, valleys,
moors and phone masts
seem dependable.

21 August

Dreams of jeopardy and twists of fate
more adrenalin than my waking hours
where I plod from shop to shop,
put my mask on, take it off.

22 August

An older white man with a beard,
a man I've never seen before, yells
'Faster!' as I run past him.

Everything begins to grate
like 'noises off' on Zoom
when nobody is muted

and the screen rebounds
to hammer drills in Oakland,
doors slammed shut in New Orleans.

23 August

With a four- and six-year-old
the day lengthens and curves
around the fields and hills

like the railway line we stare at
to await the stopping trains, the freight,
the Transpennine, the 644,

we lean on bridges, listen for the signal,
wave to drivers, rush to the rumble
of another engine coming down the track.

24 August

From Edale we walk through farms
and up a tree-lined track, eat sandwiches
beside a stream and the four-year-old says
'I'm not thinking of anything.'
Neither am I, my love, only entranced
by kestrels hovering in emerald valleys,
bees on heather breaking into flower.

25 August

Storm Francis hammers at the windows
matching my mood, irritation surging into gale force
a single out-breath the day's only refuge.

26 August

The silver birch forest
instructs me to hold fire
when instinct wants to yell
'You're wrong!'

27 August

Morning mist drenches the valley,
yellowing birch, the Derwent in full spate.
We switch the heating on,
make the season's first soup,
track infections' ascent.

28 August

Another day of solid rain
there's much to mourn
and some degrees of softening
to kind breaths in the early hours.

29 August

a new route
through fallow fields
past the stone barn
where I saw the owl

I run only in the wheel tracks
attempt to not disturb
the quiet grass
the sleeping gates

a trespasser
though pinned
and pleated
with timidity

30 August

City playgrounds open again
a distanced solitary swing
hangs in each frame.

Sunday afternoon with C
we feed ducks, watch pigeons,
cartwheel down slopes

eat the last ice-cream of summer
bike wheels turning
leaves reddening.

31 August

Final day of Eat Out to Help Out
we book dinner at the Sir William,
familiar yet odd to be served drinks,
a meal cooked by someone else.

Walking home, the Plough
and Cassiopeia in clear skies
Mars to the south,
owls on each side of the road.

September

1 September

Meditating on Manchester pavements
'with love and grief for the world'
opening my eyes now and then
to see a camera lens or passing shoes,

in good company marking
A Quiet Extinction Rebellion
alongside samba bands, Red Robes,
BLM speeches, giant silk birds.

Breathing deepens
and each sign of life
becomes a wave
inseparable from

the plane trees, lunchtime
conversations, scaffolders,
the breeze, thoughts that
rise, become entangled and release.

2 September

To Philip Larkin –
September trees thresh
just as well as May's,
full-grown, yellowing,
their wild whisper
takes my breath away.

3 September

busy roads, queues
something like rush hour

I forget face mask
jangled, unprepared
for speeding up

opening the back door
to a starlit sky
is a sprig of peace

cool draft
in fire's heart

4 September

robin
hawthorn berries
dusk

6 September

Turn to the eastern skyline
as the setting sun anoints it

and beeches take on the allure
of cypresses

at any point we could be somewhere else
careless and malleable.

5 September

I dream my eyelids are pierced with safety-pins
impossible to remove without help.
There's a connection with the urge
to be 'good', but it's long forgotten.
                                        I blether
and virtue-signal through hours of Zoom
before I see I'm quaking.

7 September

Two train journeys
coffee inside an actual café
wheeling my suitcase
among poodles
and then –
                  seagulls, sand
migrating swallows
dancing on the cliff.

So strange my bones howl
but for a while
I even forget
I'm wearing a mask.

8 September

blue sky, low tide
and I walk back and forth
on an ocean of rippled sand
until I see that fear is
trying to command the waves

returning through the trees
I glimpse the pink-red chest
of a bullfinch
on the chip shop roof

9 September

early morning jog
I misjudge the tide
and soon I'm ankle deep

later the sea goes out
and kids career
across the half-mile beach
spades in hand

in front of the laptop
I'm at the raw edge
of coherence
one floppy word
after another
like dead fish

but then I remember the toddlers
with oversize sunhats
and fistfuls of sand
learning to run

10 September

Easier to abide in fretting
than in the heart-stopping thud
that I've nothing to say.

Let writing do writing.
Stand back. Let space
and waiting do their work.

11 September

Tune to the waves (the sun gone down)
lift, curl, collapse, their bleached lips roll
from this side of the bay to that.

Seagulls grey ghosts against grey sky,
a string of pearls lighting the seafront,

turbulence and peace so close
they could find a bench to rest upon,
they could hold hands.

14 September

Mars' red eye, the four-stroke beam
of Flamborough lighthouse,
stars strung along the front
and silver skirts spread out
as evening tide recedes.

I'm meditating so hard on compassion
I barely notice there's a body here
that sways and grumbles,
marches to the sea three times a day
to feel the ground.

12 September

I've passed by many times before I see the
wooden hull, blue paint crackling, full-bellied curve.
What else below the radar? Algorithms, virus,
a red admiral on the window ledge.

13 September

Prints on low-tide sand:
a herring gull's three toes
and webbed indents,
paws, flip-flops,
trainers, worm casts.
May this step be peace.

15 September

Covid rising.
R number, cases and deaths.
A dragonfly flits
over next door's kitchen roof.
Pigeons coo and apples fall
onto the sun-warmed grass.
I take off socks, walk barefoot.
May this too become
love's instrument.

16 September

High tide, cold afternoon,
the lifeboat inflatable
practises manoeuvres.

A flock of wetsuited swimmers
with dayglo buoys waits to enter
sunless water.

Brawny herring gulls still pester food.
How can this be empty
of self, how can the one

who watches be empty and emptiness
empty too, yearning only to rise and fall
in friendliness?

17 September

I stride along tide's curves
and become fixated on the ridges,
plateaus, steep ascents
of international Covid-19 data.

18 September

Walking through the ravine
a screech owl so close by I answer it
in the way Annie taught me years ago.
Though she is dead, the dark
is instantly more passable.

19 September

Obsessing over Covid stats
before a sleepless night
tangled in sheets
or crunched into the wall.
A dawn run to the beach
finds high tide, breakers
smash against the sea wall,
furious blasts of spray
and sand-thick water.

Ruth Bader Ginsburg.
Rest in power.
Rest in peace.

20 September

Picking litter on the beach
the body of a baby seal has washed up
alongside bladderwrack,
kelp laced with fishing wire,
Haribo bags, party balloons.

21 September

gladly eating spaghetti
and watching a sleek new moon
rise and sail west

22 September

blackbird serenades the dark
above the supermarket trolleys

just before closing
mask pulled tight

23 September

At tide's edge herring gulls, half-adult
face into the wind
casually pecking crab carcasses.

24 September

I slither along rocks that surface at low tide.
Waves pound the pitted stone, the spray's
a mean baptism. Oystercatchers, sanderlings
skitter on the mossy slopes, and when the surf
booms close they trust their wings.

25 September

Arriving home
I see it through a stranger's eyes
gentle and curious
as if stepping outside time,
hoping the clock will turn back too
on Covid rising.

26 September

a moulting robin
with splodged plumage
follows me around the garden
hops onto the mower handle
snaps a fly

27 September

one of those
Sundays that stretch into the corners –
brambles thread through cow parsley, a glimpse of heron,
robin shyly rehearsing winter songs, bumblebee on sedum,
scarlet geraniums, the day gilded by the cold that
bookends it

28 September

I walk my old path in the chicken field
soothed by its familiarity but seeing
how the thinning trees have changed the light
and bracken's edged with rust.

29 September

Slamming the car door at the supermarket
silvery sculpture catches my eye – a spider's web
between wing mirror and side panel,
pristine even after twenty miles.

30 September

Raindrop orchestra
      on the umbrella
as I walk up
      and down
tensed against cold
      but tuning
to the djembe, tabla,
      tambourine,
fingertips pattering
      on fabric.

October

1 October

a patch of sun
in a city park
and it's filled
(miraculous souls)
with dancing to 'Jerusalema',
with dodgeball
and samosas

2 October

Trump tests positive.

I recall the intention
to radiate goodwill.

For some minutes
I wish him well

alongside grief
for all the lives
that patriarchs
cut down
as empires
fall.

3 October

Treetop walkways
& zipwires
in the rain
with the kids
hot chocolate
& birthday cake
& driving home
singing
'Now that it's raining more than ever
Know that we'll still have each other
You can stand under my umbrella ...'

4 October

                    I pause
from dead-heading calendula,
sensing air infused with voices –

long-tailed tits
        this branch
                then that

don't scurry from joy
let it alight, feathered,
buoyant in my palms.

5 October

Flooding in the Midlands //

fires in Oregon //

Trump in or out of hospital //

the MP who insists
the government is closely monitoring
arms sales to Saudi //

I stay over-busy
hence detached, elated
absent-mindedly unkind

6 October

Bustling from shop to shop
tempted and
forgetting.

Time between bells
to pause
and listen.

This week's Star Baker
makes a Dharma wheel
in dough.

7 October

Meeting in the kitchen at workday's end
we compare Zoom meetings
and discuss the R number.
I throw all the vegetables into a soup pot
and add nuts. Paths thicken with leaves.

105

8 October

rush & push
push & rush
does not distract
from pounding head
only enflames it
as I zip
from screen
to screen

9 October

Dream of baking potatoes
in Tara Brach's kitchen.

Cases doubling every two weeks,
local lockdown coming soon.

The cat pukes and wees everywhere.
We light winter's first fire.
I can smell tatties.

10 October

Negative mood sets in
& colours the screen.
Glued to the spot
by impatience
I forget how to move
how to walk out
into rain.

11 October

stock-still in the sunny garden
pleasure grows to gladness
but vanishes when I consider
how to describe it
                    pause again
try to be a wordless sponge
the robin devours a worm
sleepy drone-flies
land on sedum

12 October

When they announce 'new tiers in place'
like many listening I hear 'tears'
and picture the Cabinet
drying their eyes
collective sorrow
full consent to weep
in public places.

13 October

Pain lifts and I spring up
like a loosed balloon
blether and chortle
at mute screen-bound faces.

14 October

chanting the Great Compassion Mantra
though I don't know what the words mean
or even what language they're in
they resound through my sternum
till I'm tranced into being present
                    plugged into
                              something
I'd like to call the end of hate, no second term
for Trump, and boundless peace

in the messy kitchen as rain pounds the decking
and lockdown strides closer I chant
and chant because at this point
everything that can be done
must be done

15 October

Tabs the cat recovers from a UTI
and two nights at vet hospital.
She comes home skinny, thirsty
with no appetite and we take turns
to let her sleep in our laps
till our legs go numb, heating on high,
urgent tasks undone.

16 October

hyper-vigilant about the cat –
how many sips of water, bites of tuna

and I turn vigilant about my short-comings
so even hyphenated words are shameful

the cat stretches her shaky body
and curls up again, no disguise

17 October

Squirrels intent on harvest,
acorns, sweet chestnuts
detached and falling.

Can there be truce with decay.
We kiss at the kissing gate.
Tabs eats a few morsels.

Another retreat begins –
a new flavour of Zoom boxes,
an out-breath.

18 October

Tabs sniffs her food & walks away
breathe with worry, with tenderness
breathe with her settling on our laps
and you stroking the softest fur
behind her ears, breathe with the heart
that's frantic to do the right thing
whatever the thing is that will keep the cat alive
or earn a big tick-box in the sky.

19 October

I miss the scheduled meeting
& discovering my error tears bubble
and I scrabble to explain

my feet take me to the village shop
where the kindness of almost-strangers
and a cup of tea makes the day new

20 October

I'm in love with Autumn
won't hear a word against her

sheep field's russet and sage
dusk's lingering bouquet

paths remade hourly
with gold and crimson

deciduous hillsides
tarragon and caramel

let's tread the falling leaves
and weave a gorgeous tweed

to warm us into winter

21 October

After long days of Zoom
the final room is closed,
I take your hand and walk
into the night. Will the stars
be in their places when we're
long gone? We pitch a guess.
For a while the lane is
beautifully absent of certainty.

22 October

another record number of cases

I gobble news
link after link

as if I'll finally click through
to an end of Covid

23 October

on the edge of
moving into Tier 3

walking to the car
Covid-fear judders over me

nervous in shops
I do the distanced dance-step

but still haven't figured how to stop
my glasses steaming up

24 October

watching *The Social Dilemma*
    fear for the kids
    for all of us
compelled by algorithms

summon kindness
    for the shaking heart
    shallow breath
the hand that reaches for a screen

25 October

David Attenborough's Witness Statement.
I'm quick to believe horror, slow to hope.
Can we stave off mass extinction
by growing crops vertically,
making deserts into solar farms?

Tawny owls call from the woods,
an oak tree has self-seeded in the lawn.

26 October

The clocks gone back
now-hail, now-brief
sunburst, now-rain
of one degree
warmer, heading
for one point five
that makes the windows
waterfalls, the paths
impassable. Where's
kindness here?
Dread hooks its fingers,
primes the system
for catastrophe.

27 October

Run / half-run / walk
up the hill
in drizzle
stopping
to admire
the gracious beech
and chestnut
with their
golden, rusty gowns

I've unsubscribed
from all news channels
except this –
the slow and glorious.

28 October

Nausea and headache return
No energy | I ignore
Push through | Meet deadlines

Is it Long Covid | Something else
Should I bother the GP

29 October

Fields saturated
sheep like lumpy ancient quilts

rain coming down
and Covid going up

France on brink of lockdown

everything's different today
but I can't work it out

and everything's the same
[I Zoom, walk with chickens,
chop vegetables, and cleave,
yes, to the sunnier side of gloom]

30 October

Tabs is full of beans again
leaps onto the bed at 6 a.m.

the robin sings and I whisper
mettā phrases out of desperation

but they filter through
into the morning

running water
may all beings be well

brushing teeth
may we be safe

and tonight
a full moon rises

like a blessing
over half-leaved woods.

31 October

I hold my covid-grown ponytail
above my head
and slice through it
with the kitchen scissors.

Johnson announces
a second lockdown.

November

1 November

Murmuring
'May all beings be safe and well'
as Storm A and Hurricane Z
batter the windows.

2 November

A simple joy slips into finger-holds and crevices
and builds from many sources – long-tailed tits
wittering in silver birch, clusters of nitrous
bonnet-caps, a beech limb rippling
with curtain fungus, light filtered
through a lacy canopy – I let it grow,
keep out the news, keep in new knowledge
that the acorns underfoot are raining down
from oak trees everywhere. Plentiful. A mast year.

3 November

I hold at bay the thought
'What if he wins?'

until midnight & I'm zapping
from one headline to the next

terror condenses in my solar plexus
shudders out through ribs & guts
& arms until I imagine taking up arms

4 November

You come back in to say
Radio 4 thinks Trump is going to win

it's sunnier than it's been for weeks
I walk into the blue and gold

lean against an oak who weaves a tapestry
of leaves and acorn cups

nuthatches bob and nip
along the branches

I speak to the trees for hours
they reply

5 November

Two hot chocolates
a walk in the woods
another day of no-news
and I'm giddy with joy.
An owl hoots nearby
the constellations dazzle
and I vow to believe the impossible,
the end will come soon enough
why not dare love to occupy each cell.

6 November

Once I look at news I'm lost
jabbing at headlines
and the pulsating red LIVE button
till my nervous system is pulsating
eyes reddened, headache brewing.

7 November

The trees lose all their leaves
but they're not dead

in summer they make food
from light and water

we stare at them
across the playground

and nothing is
unworthy of awe.

8 November

it looks like an election result
but fear triggers in from the side-lines
I want to stop time
at Kamala Harris' speech
and fast-forward to a happy ending
or at least no collateral deaths

9 November

Pfizer announce possible breakthrough
I surf the stats, length of trials
number of participants
vaccine inequality
billions of doses
projected cost
this year
next

mutations

what do I know?
the sweet gloominess of dusk
mist blanketing the hills
tawny owls' duet
watching the dark
come to the window
and offer me its hand

10 November

never a good idea to read about QAnon
before bed or the televangelist
who blames Covid on queers

something medieval about these times
the fourteenth century on amphetamines

11 November

biscuits and more biscuits
till sugar-buzzed
I lay into the inbox

hours later it's undefeated
and I've forgotten what better use
to make of days diminishing

12 November

I take refuge in cake
soon I'm full of it
and empty of words

13 November

Another week ends
another record number of infections

another forty-eight days till Brexit
another day Trump does not concede

another attempt
to face the past with forgiveness

the future with grace.

14 November

the outside never as gloomy
as it seems from inside
even in drizzle it's lighter, wider
and a nest in the thicket
is finally visible

15 November

Waking to a chorus of the blues
I run from it into the squall's teeth,
dodging rain and cowpats.

Later I scrape leaves
kindle patience to pick them out
between the stones.

Turn my back and more have fallen.
This is how it is.
I'd like a giant receiving dish

to blossom from my spine
that harkens only
to the robin's winter song.

16 November

paths diverge –

this one the mean observation
    that leaps from the tongue
    is spoken aloud
    and savoured
    grows into gossip
    fattens into action
    or inaction

the other a cruel thought
    that's held in the mouth
    watched over
    and let be
    till it calms
    fades
    is forgotten

17 November

My heart tries to beat its way out
and sleep stays arms-length all night.

I'm craving the split-second of sugar hit
though it's to blame. I bit and bit
chunks of treacle so sweet it was indeed bitter.

Beneath the need to bite and swallow
a clean sorrow will not disclose its root.

18 November

A minute to relish new moon
in rain-spattered sky, remnant
of pink-grey light on the horizon
before clouds devour it.

An evening for hot chocolate and fire,
leaning back from being busy
and important; the slap of 'not good,
nowhere good enough' biding its time.

19 November

sunlight
a ladybird
the clematis re-flowering

and a clear night
zero-ing the air
hollowing breath

20 November

mist and low cloud
droop across the window
like old curtains

nausea is back

I embed myself in screens
greedy for a recipe
or New Season

21 November

Can it be true
there's nothing left to say
I've run out of words
a month or more to go?

22 November

attempt to run away
from painful hip
and end up at a limp

nothing quenches
the low-lying cloud
that slowly drowns the day

I'm out of love with Netflix
and keep stabbing
at my phone

before I remember
I've deleted
the news app

23 November

no app

so I flick on the lunchtime news
which is good
    "the AstraZeneca vaccine"
and bad
    "the last time CO_2 levels were this high
    the planet was three degrees warmer"
what to do

make the day's first thoughts
soothe rather than strangle

tune the body mountainwards

act

24 November

At 1.30 a.m. I'm at the back door
in my nightie videoing heavy machinery.
John from Network Rail Complaints
listens patiently and logs my ranting.

Lack of sleep haunts the day,
claws at confidence
till I stutter and forget
my train of thought. Solace

of the *Bake Off* final with a roaring stove,
what will we do without words like
choux, chiffon, ganache to mark the weeks
and roll around our mouths?

27 November

is it good enough
is this good enough
are you
are they
is she

a rock of no good
rattles round
at 1, 2, 3 a.m.
alongside any number
of bad moves

25 November

sick as a dog
and underneath the sickness
a low, slow grieving

the GP says
no antibody tests
are available

26 November

We re-roof the shed.
I hammer in the last nails
as darkness falls
and you drive to the chippy.

28 November

Where brook meets river
I halt beside the currents

a rusty-bellied bird
catches my eye

could be a dipper
but it arrows

across water
emerald flashes

as it tilts
and blue-green

dashes upstream.
The day's murk-filled

but the kingfisher
lights hours beyond its measure.

29 November

Running through mist and mud
are these days always so short?

Clouds lift for half an hour
in the afternoon

with a stranger's kindness
finding and returning a lost phone.

30 November

Arriving in the Zoom room
floored with weariness
though these are friends
whose company I relish,
I switch off camera, listen
only from the corners of my ears.

I want to simply hang out
in the lunch queue, on the street
or in a corridor, drink tea,
chat over food, lean forward
laughing, not caring how close we get
or whose breath meets whose.

December

1 December

first heavy frost
says Winter
in its pale-blue cloak

a drowsy fly meanders
through the door ajar
on midday sun

I walk under clouds' lattice
gazing
at magnitude

for now
let's turn the dial
away from fault-finding

2 December

Grateful for a rainless track
the Plough, Orion
waxing moon

for tears that spill
from sleepless nights
and crack the heart

to let love –
or what's beyond love –
out.

3 December

beyond a hot-water bottle
blanket and chocolate
any instinct for self-care
seems to have evaporated

4 December

Snow edges trees
picks out
new angles

I sit sideways to Zoom
hoping to look attentive
but captivated by the blots

and blats that sweep
and whiten sky.
Let's take off this

oh-so-grown-up talk
roll it into snowballs
shriek and slither.

5 December

My acquaintance with three a.m.
renews and deepens
but it's not a healthy friendship

heart a wrecking ball
mind a breaker's yard

for seconds I gather it in –
soften shoulders
but soon we're off

in manic quickstep
to the Land of
Never Sleep Again.

6 December

Eight hours sleep
a run, a shower, meditation,
toast and tea, a bike ride
to the park and I feel
relatively sane

grateful for Michel Barnier
'We must remain calm'
for opposable thumbs
and the ability to switch off
the radio.

7 December

Grey heron lances upstream
between the riverbanks
as I slump-step through
Monday morning.

She opens a gap in gloom
and later for the sun to pierce
through late afternoon
when there's the usual mix

of disbelief and chocolate.

I'm violently allergic to the words
'Brexit Trade Talks'.

8 December

They're calling it V Day
first vaccine rollouts.

A government minister
sheds tears.

Sharp stabs
of wintry rain.

Inbox shrinks, expands.
I cook a heap of sag aloo and rice.

My feet stay cold.
The neighbour's cockerel crows at midnight.

9 December

What does it mean to hold myself dear
as I run through rain
past rushing burn
where ten crows rise?

It means to stop and tend the aching hip
then continue gently
holding dear the feet, the dancing step,
the eyes, pausing at hill's crest

to scan the valley
which is Middle-earth today –
Mam Tor loosening its grip on clouds
and strips of gauzy mist

caught on far pines
skies opening towards White Peak –
holding dear the muddy air,
the humbling gift.

10 December

A day of sliding rooms
five a.m. sitting in bed
to meditate, driving
to the Post Office at nine
then Zoom to Zoom
and WhatsApp video.

Day fades
before I get outside.
It may sound like
I know what I'm doing
but it's a mix of pinball
and aimless floating.

11 December

Probably a mistake
to attempt
all the Christmas errands
in one day.

Frustration at queues
fear at crowds
but almost impossible
to just stop

and buy
nothing.

12 December

Walking the edge
between
good enough
and over-reaching

I haver back and forth
lean towards 'too much'
like pushing a wobbly tooth
and getting spurts of pain.

What is self-care
without collapse?
What is compassion
without stretch and ache?

Where's the place for risk
and the wild one
who dances her heart out
at the pier's end?

13 December

Writing cards & breathing love
into stock phrases

Draping the house with lights
until it shimmers

Listening to 'The Messiah'
and 'ye shall find rest unto your soul'

14 December

bird flu
the chickens
must stay cooped up

meantime
London enters Tier 3
& there's a new mutation

we debate how, when,
& where to bubble
& consider calling it off

15 December

I pass the meeting room,
empty and closed.

Driving there and back on wintry evenings
seems unthinkable.

I miss the fellow bodies
but I love this practice

in the very midst – same old hoodie,
stained cushions, tea cooling.

16 December

breaths of night air
at the five-barred gate
no Saturn-Jupiter conjunction visible

I fry up broccoli pakoras
we laugh out loud at *Derry Girls*
and dream of trifle

I'm glad I don't have to live
on thirty-seven pounds a week

17 December

muzzy-head
a common cold?
lingering and taking root

why do I think
clearing the inbox
will cure all?

come and stand
in the winter sun my love
splash in the puddles

18 December

Ignoring myself all day
Passing by on the other side of the street
Ashamed, with nothing to give
And the rain relentless.

19 December

Boris
flanked by Chris and Patrick:
new variant

new Tier 4
less Christmas
no Christmas.

We cancel things
make empty promises.

Bracken's receded
and the rock
that gets late sun

is visible again.
I perch there, listening
to a podcast on charisma.

20 December

Mid-run the hill-stream stops me
in my tracks with water's

accidental, un-made melody.
Later we shimmy to the Salvation Army

playing 'Jingle Bells' in Weston Park,
sing distanced carols near the twilit church

then catch The Lovenotes on YouTube. Amen
to music's sustenance these months.

21 December

solstice
& in the northern hemisphere
the day

imperceptibly
begins
to lengthen

the valley
stays
shrouded

lorries
tailback
through Kent

borders
remain
closed

turning
to the
body

kindness
imperceptibly
lengthens

22 December

item after item
errand after errand
shop after shop
sanitiser after sanitiser

what if I don't find
chocolate coins
a gift for X or Y

I savour nausea's absence
grateful not to be a lorry driver

23 December

Wet and warm, everything puddled,
drains bursting, brook in spate.
Plod home drenched from a walk
to the shop. Chickens huddle
or strut about bedraggled. I peel tape
from frayed paper, sing along to The Ukes,
glimpses of holiday, ready
to take the foot off the pedal.

24 December

When the days are too full
to go to the woods
poems wither
before they reach the page.

25 December

Grateful for my beloved who stays steady
and takes me in her arms mid-morning
between spuds and sprouts.
Grateful for a muddy walk with a collie
and an eight-year-old. Glad for fires
to gather round outside with friends,
for glow-in-the-dark bouncy balls,
for vegan pigs-in-duvets, for tiaras,
and gravy made and frozen in advance.

26 December

Catch up on tasks
sort leftovers
promise
to stop
gather awareness
listen
but snacks and TV
get
the upper hand.
And the storm
lashes windows
almost drowning out
the quiet voice:
begin again
and then again begin.

27 December

hello nausea
hello headache
hello eye pain
restlessness and tiredness
roll into one
get up
lie down
lie down
get up
take pills

sometimes distraction is
kindness
and sometimes kindness
is giving up
or trying to keep
softening impatience
as it builds and flares
in every
particle of skin

28 December

The kindest place today
is climbing Millstone Edge
clinging to heather
leaning into rock

grass doubled
with frost
icy branches
creaking in slow fog

we make it to the top
you gather rusty cans
remnants of Haribo
and dog poo bags

there's always more –
stuff in the mind
stuff thrown away
as best we can

we pick it up
try not to swear
at long-gone carelessness
move on.

29 December

Ending the year
as it began
on retreat
and I'm no less
in need of
reminders.
Bound
to the spinning wheel
of grumpiness.
Impermanence
a distant refuge.
The paltry mantra
of 'This too shall pass'.

30 December

The more I tell myself to calm
the more my skin jitters.
As Tier 4 sidles closer,
infections increase
and friends sicken,
I seek salvation in
the truffles that vow
'You choose the moment
we'll provide the bliss'.

31 December

What does the last day have to say?
For auld lang syne my dear.
At this very minute Brexit happens,
Covid deaths soar, WhatsApp buzzes
with flowers, fireworks, with drones
glowing poems over Edinburgh,
with friendship.
                              Thank you
for this ship, the crazy ride where love itself
became the journey and the tide.

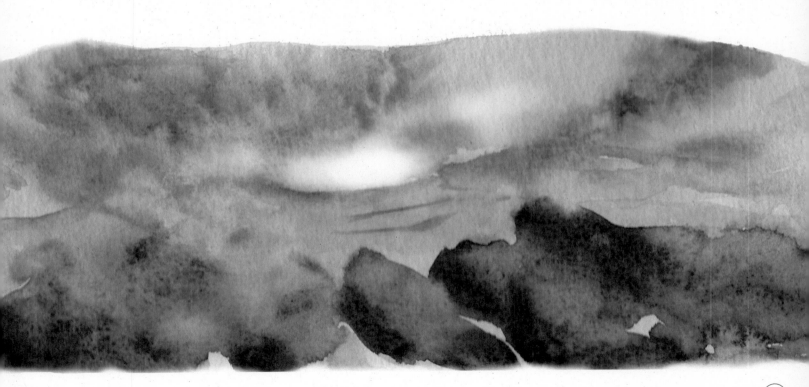

Acknowledgements

Earlier versions of some of these poems were first published in *The North* magazine.

Thank you to Fiona, whose love, steadiness and companionship steered me through this year. Thank you to the families and communities I have the good fortune to belong to, and whose presence weaves through these poems: friends and neighbours in Upper Padley; the LASS fam; the iBme crew; friends and colleagues at Bodhi College and Gaia House; The Poetry Business; the Woltons, the Outrams and Rowbothams; dear family-friends Martine and Cherisa; Lu and Kat; the Beautiful Beasties and the Old Pals.

Thank you to Venerable Candā whose invitation to set an intention for 2020 planted the seed for this project.

Thank you to Helen Lyle who gave me the small, square, orange, spiral-bound notebook called 'Zap', that I reached for at the end of each day.

Thank you to Robert Hamberger, loyal friend and poetry companion, whose patient, careful and loving feedback was invaluable.

Thank you to Emma Burleigh and Francesca Romano, for their creativity and inspiration in co-creating this book.

References

'Was it for this the clay grew tall?' from *Futility* by Wilfred Owen, written in May 1918.

Parasite (2019), directed by Bong Joon-ho [feature film].

Planet of the Humans (2019), directed by Jeff Gibbs [documentary film].

Queer Eye: More than a Makeover (2018–present), Scout Productions/Netflix [Reality TV series].

Juneteenth: the anniversary of 19 June 1865, when enslaved African Americans were informed about the Emancipation Proclamation in Texas more than two years after it was signed.

I Am Not Your Negro (2016), directed by Raoul Peck [documentary film].

The Limits to Growth. 1972 report on exponential population and economic growth with a finite supply of resources.

Resmaa Menakem, *My Grandmother's Hands: Racialised Trauma and the Pathway to Mending Our Hearts and Bodies*, Penguin, 2021.

'Jerusalema' (2019), hit single by South African DJ and record producer Master KG featuring vocalist Nomcebo Zikode. A video of an accompanying dance challenge, attributed to a group of Angolan friends, went viral in 2020.

'Now that it's raining more than ever …' from 'Umbrella' sung by Rihanna (2007).

The Social Dilemma (2020), directed by Jeff Orlowski [docudrama].

A Life on Our Planet: My Witness Statement (2020), documentary narrated by David Attenborough.

About

River Wolton – the author

River Wolton is a former Derbyshire Poet Laureate whose previous collections include *Leap* and *Indoor Skydiving*. She has led writing and arts projects for more than twenty years in schools and community projects. River has completed Dharma teacher training with Bodhi College, and teaches meditation retreats at Gaia House, Devon, and with groups throughout the UK.

You can find out more about her at www.riverwolton.co.uk

Emma Burleigh – the illustrator

Emma Burleigh is an artist and illustrator with a passion for watercolour and a deep love of nature. She is also a meditator. Her previous publications include *Soul Color: a ten week watercolour course-book for mindfulness and creativity* and *Earth Color: an eight week mixed media art course-book for nature connection* both published by Liminal 11.

You can find out more about her at www.emmaburleigh.com

Francesca Romano – the designer

Francesca Romano is a graphic designer with an MA in Book Design. She previously worked at the Oxford University Press and has been an independent designer since 2019. She is interested in reading and publishing practices and also teaches at the University of Reading.

You can see more of her work at francescaromano.co.uk